TEAM SPIRIT

SMART BOOKS FOR YOUNG FANS

S0-AEY-761

THE COLORADO AVALANCHE

BY

MARK STEWART

CONTENT CONSULTANT
DENIS GIBBONS
SOCIETY FOR INTERNATIONAL HOCKEY RESEARCH

NORWOOD HOUSE PRESS

CHICAGO, ILLINOIS

Norwood House Press
P.O. Box 316598
Chicago, Illinois 60631

For information regarding Norwood House Press, please visit our website at:
www.norwoodhousepress.com or call 866-565-2900.

All photos courtesy of Associated Press except the following:
Imperial Tobacco (6), O-Pee-Chee Ltd. (7, 21),
Getty Images (8, 9, 12, 17, 19, 22, 25, 27, 28, 32, 35 bottom, 37, 39, 43), Beckett Publications (10, 18, 31),
Author's Collection (11, 33), Topps, Inc. (15, 35 top right, 45), The Upper Deck Company (23),
TIME Inc./Sports Illustrated for Kids (30), Tag Express (34), The Sporting News (35 top left),
Hockey Illustrated, Inc. (38), Parkhurst Products (40), The World Hockey Association (42 top),
The National Hockey League (42 bottom), Pinnacle Brands (43 top).
Cover Photo: AP Photo/The Canadian Press, Trevor Hagan

The memorabilia and artifacts pictured in this book are presented for educational and informational purposes,
and come from the collection of the author.

Editor: Mike Kennedy
Designer: Ron Jaffe
Project Management: Black Book Partners, LLC.
Special thanks to Topps, Inc.

Library of Congress Cataloging-in-Publication Data

Stewart, Mark, 1960 July 7-
  The Colorado Avalanche / by Mark Stewart. -- Revised edition.
      pages cm. -- (Team spirit)
  Includes bibliographical references and index.
  Summary: "A revised Team Spirit Hockey edition featuring the Colorado
Avalanche that chronicles the history and accomplishments of the team.
Includes access to the Team Spirit website which provides additional
information and photos"-- Provided by publisher.
   ISBN 978-1-59953-618-7 (library edition : alk. paper) -- ISBN
978-1-60357-626-0 (ebook) 1. Colorado Avalanche (Hockey
team)--History--Juvenile literature. 2. Hockey
teams--Colorado--History--Juvenile literature. I. Title.
   GV848.C65S84 2014
   796.962'640978883--dc23
                                                                          2013034231

Manufactured in the United States of America in Stevens Point, Wisconsin.
239N—012014

COVER PHOTO: The Avs gather to celebrate a goal during the 2012–13 season.

TABLE OF CONTENTS

ABOUT OUR GLOSSARY

In this book, there may be several words that you are reading for the first time. Some are sports words, some are new vocabulary words, and some are familiar words that are used in an unusual way. All of these words are defined on page 46. Throughout the book, sports words appear in **bold type**. Regular vocabulary words appear in ***bold italic type***.

MEET THE AVALANCHE

How long does a sports team need to play in a city before it can call that city home? The players on the Colorado Avalanche wondered this when the team moved from Quebec City in Canada to Denver, Colorado. That question was answered at the end of their first season, when the "Avs" won hockey's greatest prize, the **Stanley Cup**. They have been treated like family ever since.

The Avalanche began their hockey journey in the 1970s. Back then, they had a different name—Nordiques—and many of their fans spoke a different language—French. The team was located in Canada and played in a different league.

This book tells the story of the Avalanche. Today, they are as much a part of the Colorado landscape as the Rocky Mountains. Fans travel from all over the region to watch them play. When the Avalanche get rolling, they truly live up to their name. At their best, there's simply no stopping them.

Gabriel Landeskog congratulates goalie Semyon Varlamov after a victory.

GLORY DAYS

Hockey has been a **professional** sport in North America since the early 1900s. Over the years, there have been several professional leagues. Some were major leagues—including the **National Hockey League (NHL)**—and some were **minor leagues**. As long as fans were willing to buy tickets, there was always a chance to start a new team or a new league.

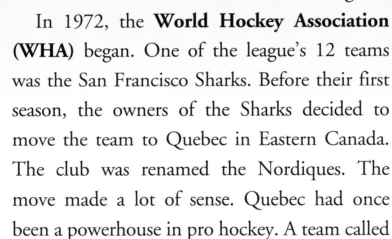

JOE MALONE

In 1972, the **World Hockey Association (WHA)** began. One of the league's 12 teams was the San Francisco Sharks. Before their first season, the owners of the Sharks decided to move the team to Quebec in Eastern Canada. The club was renamed the Nordiques. The move made a lot of sense. Quebec had once been a powerhouse in pro hockey. A team called the Bulldogs won the Stanley Cup twice, in 1912 and again in 1913. Their leader was a legendary goal-scorer named Joe Malone.

The WHA was made up of hungry young players, as well as a few stars who left the NHL to make more money. The first leader of the Nordiques was J.C. Tremblay. He had played in the NHL **All-Star Game** seven times with the Montreal Canadiens. Quebec filled out its lineup with emerging stars such as Rejean Houle, Marc Tardif, Serge Bernier, Christian Bordeleau, Richard Brodeur, Jamie Hislop, and Réal Cloutier. All but Brodeur and Cloutier had seen ice time in the NHL.

The Nordiques played twice for the WHA championship. They lost in 1975 and won in 1977. In 1979, the Nordiques were invited to join the NHL, along with three other WHA teams. Facing new competition, a fresh group of stars led the "Nords." One of them was Michel Goulet, who grew up in Quebec. There was also Dale Hunter and the Stastny brothers—Peter, Marian, and Anton. They all helped the team reach the finals of the

LEFT: Joe Malone was one of the first major hockey stars in Quebec.
ABOVE: J.C. Tremblay was a good leader and a great passer.

Eastern **Conference** in 1984–85 and earn a **division** championship in 1985–86. Also during this time, the Nordiques developed a fierce rivalry with the Canadiens, who played just three hours away, in Montreal.

In the early 1990s, Quebec welcomed more young stars, including Joe Sakic, Adam Foote, Owen Nolan, Valeri Kamensky, and Mats Sundin. In 1991, the team **drafted** Eric Lindros, who was expected to be hockey's next superstar. When Lindros made it clear that he did not want to play for the Nordiques, they traded him for a package of talented players, including Peter Forsberg and Mike Ricci. In one year, the team went from 20 wins to 47!

Despite their success, the Nordiques were forced to find a new home. Quebec City simply wasn't large enough to support the team. After the 1994–95 season, the club moved to Denver, a city filled with fans who loved hockey, and was renamed the Avalanche. Many years earlier, an NHL team called the Rockies had played there. That team moved to New Jersey and became the Devils.

LEFT: Joe Sakic spent his entire 21–year career with the Nordiques and the Avs.   **ABOVE**: Peter Forsberg combined with Sakic to give Colorado a great one-two scoring punch.

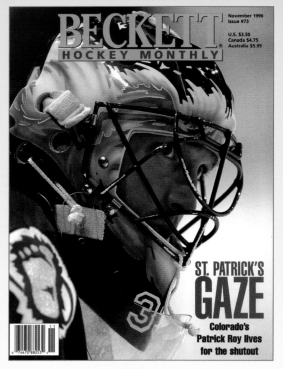

The Avs found success immediately. In 1995–96, they reached the **Stanley Cup Finals**. Sakic and superstar goalie Patrick Roy—who joined the team during the season—led Colorado to a four-game sweep of the Florida Panthers. In 2000–01, the Avs won the Stanley Cup again.

Year in and year out, Colorado kept winning games and bringing exciting new players to the ice. Some were already stars when they joined the team, including Claude Lemieux, Rob Blake, Sandis Ozolinsh, and Ray Bourque. Others—such as Adam Deadmarsh, Milan Hejduk, Chris Drury, and Alex Tanguay—started their careers with the club. No matter who was wearing the Colorado uniform, they knew what it took to play championship hockey. The fans appreciated their effort and skill. During one stretch, the team sold out nearly 500 games in a row.

In 2005, the NHL made new rules that limited player salaries for every team. This created some tough decisions for the Avalanche. In order to keep leaders such as Sakic and Blake in the lineup, the team had to part ways with popular **veterans**, including Forsberg. When

Sakic retired in 2009 after 21 years with the team, it marked the end of one amazing *era* and the beginning of another.

Not surprisingly, the team struggled after losing Sakic. Beginning in 2008–09, the Avs missed the **playoffs** four times in five seasons. They had good players—including Foote, Paul Stastny (Peter's son), Marek Svatos, and John-Michael Liles—but rebuilding takes time. This is something Colorado fans had never experienced. Incredibly, before the 2008–09 season, the team had not had one losing season since arriving from Canada.

The club's patience started paying off a few years later, when more young talent joined the **roster**. Left wing Gabriel Landeskog was named team captain at age 20. Center Matt Duchene was picked for the All-Star Game. The Avs got goalie Semyon Varlamov in a trade. Meanwhile, future stars such as Nathan MacKinnon were poised to move into the starting lineup. Colorado fans know it's only a matter of time before the Stanley Cup is within their grasp once more.

LEFT: Patrick Roy made headlines when he joined the Avs.
ABOVE: Paul Stastny and Matt Duchene brought new energy to Colorado.

HOME ICE

During the team's years in Canada, its home was the Quebec Coliseum, which was one of the larger arenas in pro hockey. When the Avalanche arrived in Colorado in 1995, they played in the McNichols Sports Arena. The "Big Mac" had been home to the Denver Spurs of the WHA. During the 1970s and 1980s, the Colorado Rockies of the NHL also played there.

In 1999, the Avalanche moved into a new arena. Colorado fans nicknamed it "The Can" after the soft drink company that helped build it. In 2008, the arena was home to the Democratic National Convention. During the convention, Barack Obama was officially chosen to run for president.

BY THE NUMBERS

- *There are 18,007 seats for hockey in Colorado's arena.*

- *As of the 2013–14 season, the Avalanche had retired the numbers of five players: 19 (Joe Sakic), 21 (Peter Forsberg), 33 (Patrick Roy), 52 (Adam Foote), and 77 (Ray Bourque).*

- *The Nordiques retired the numbers of four players: 3 (J.C. Tremblay), 8 (Marc Tardif), 16 (Michel Goulet), and 26 (Peter Stastny).*

The players and fans stand for the National Anthem before a game in Colorado's arena.

Colorado's team colors are blue, white, and a deep red known as burgundy. The Avs have also used black and silver in their uniform design. The team's *logo* features a mountain peak in the shape of the letter *A*, with snow swooshing down behind a hockey puck. The players wear their dark uniforms for home games and their white ones for away games.

During their 23 seasons in Quebec, the Nordiques wore a blue and white uniform. It included the fleur-de-lis, which is an ancient symbol used by French kings and queens. The uniform also had a bright red letter *N* next to a hockey stick. A lot of fans thought it looked like an elephant!

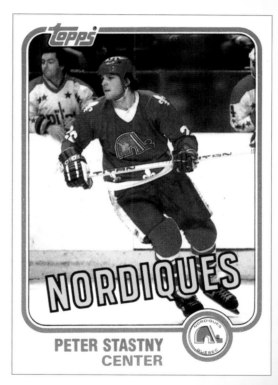

NORDIQUES

PETER STASTNY
CENTER

LEFT: P.A. Parenteau celebrates a goal in Colorado's 2012–13 away uniform. **ABOVE**: The fleur-de-lis can be seen on the sleeves of Peter Stastny's jersey from the 1980s.

Before the Avs ever skated in Colorado, the team already knew something about championship hockey. Indeed, the club's first title came in 1977, when it was the Nordiques and was part of the World Hockey Association. Quebec's top scorers were Réal Cloutier, Marc Tardif, Serge Bernier, and the Bordeleau brothers, Christian and Paulin. The defense was led by J.C. Tremblay and Jim Dorey, and backed by goalie Richard Brodeur.

The Nordiques advanced through the first two rounds of the playoffs. Next, they faced the Winnipeg Jets in the WHA Finals. With Tardif and Tremblay slowed by injuries, Bernier stepped up and played like a superstar. The series went the distance. Quebec hosted Game 7 with a chance to win the championship on its home ice. With their fans rooting them on, the Nordiques skated to an 8–2 victory to capture the WHA title.

The team's first NHL championship came soon after its move from Quebec to Colorado, in 1996. Joe Sakic had a terrific year for the Avalanche. He led the club with 51 goals and 69 **assists**.

The Avs win the 1996 Stanley Cup—let the celebration begin!

The team's best playmaker was Peter Forsberg, who had 86 assists. Colorado had several other top players, including forwards Valeri Kamensky and Claude Lemieux, defensemen Uwe Krupp and Sandis Ozolinsh, and goalie Patrick Roy.

The Avalanche faced the Florida Panthers in the Stanley Cup Finals. Colorado took the first three games thanks to the great goaltending of Roy. The Panthers scored just four times in those games. Roy was even better in Game 4. He turned aside shot after shot. But so did Florida goalie John Vanbiesbrouck. Neither team could score in the first 60 minutes. The game remained a scoreless tie after the first **overtime** and then after the second overtime, too.

Finally, in the third overtime, Krupp scored to win the game. Fans were amazed when they saw the stats. The Panthers had fired 63 shots on goal, and Roy had stopped every one. The Conn Smythe Trophy for **Most Valuable Player (MVP)** of the playoffs went to Sakic. He led all players with 18 goals. Six of them were game-winners.

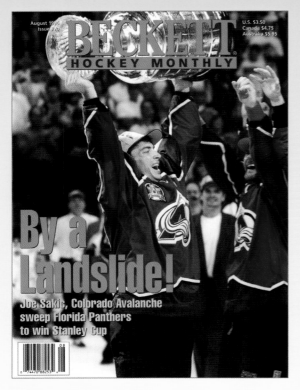

August 1996
Issue #70

BECKETT
HOCKEY MONTHLY

U.S. $3.50
Canada $4.75
Australia $5.95

By a
Landslide!

Joe Sakic, Colorado Avalanche
sweep Florida Panthers
to win Stanley Cup

Colorado's second Stanley Cup came five years later. New to the team were forwards Milan Hejduk, Alex Tanguay, and Chris Drury, as well as defensemen Rob Blake and Ray Bourque. They helped the Avalanche produce the best record in the NHL.

As the playoffs started, the Avs had extra **motivation**. Colorado's players and fans desperately wanted Bourque to win a championship. He had played for 21 seasons in the NHL, but the Stanley Cup had always **eluded** him. He joined the Avalanche in 2000, hoping for one last chance at the title.

This time, Colorado's opponent in the finals was the New Jersey Devils. Colorado fans knew it would not be an easy series. For one thing, Forsberg was nursing an injury. Even worse, the Devils had won the Stanley Cup the year before. Their goalie, Martin Brodeur, was fantastic.

Brodeur, however, was not ready for the Avalanche in Game 1. They won 5–0. Sakic skated circles around the New Jersey defense, while Roy was sensational in goal. The Devils bounced back and took the lead in the series. The Avs traveled to New Jersey for

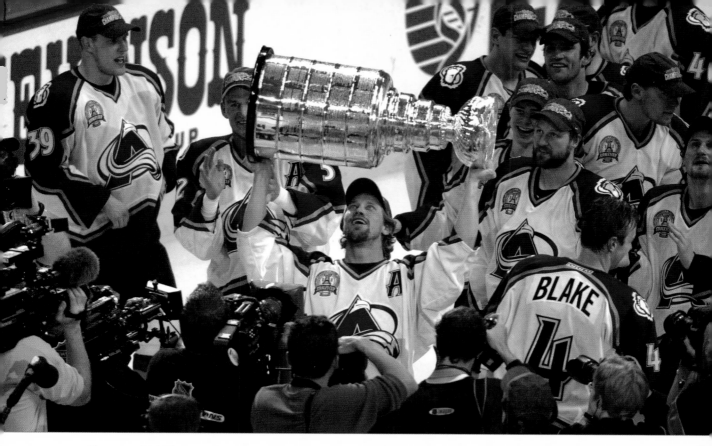

Game 6. The pressure was on Roy and his teammates. They had to win two games in a row to capture the Stanley Cup.

Roy picked the perfect time to be perfect. Nothing the Devils tried in Game 6 worked. Roy stopped 24 shots for a 4–0 victory. The series moved back to Colorado for Game 7. The Devils kept a close watch on Colorado's top scorers. But Tanguay still found room to skate. The 21-year-old snapped two shots past Brodeur, and Sakic added a third goal. Colorado won 3–1. The Avs were Stanley Cup champions for the second time.

LEFT: Joe Sakic raises the Stanley Cup in 1996. He was also a key contributor to the team's second championship.
ABOVE: Peter Forsberg gets his chance to carry the Stanley Cup in 2001.

GO-TO GUYS

To be a true star in the NHL, you need more than a great slapshot. You have to be a "go-to guy"—someone teammates trust to make the winning play when the seconds are ticking away in a big game. Fans in Quebec and Colorado have had a lot to cheer about over the years, including these great stars …

THE PIONEERS

J.C. TREMBLAY   Defenseman

• BORN: 1/22/1939 • DIED: 12/7/1994 • PLAYED FOR TEAM: 1972–73 TO 1978–79

Jean-Claude "J.C." Tremblay was Quebec's first star. During the 1960s, he had been one of the NHL's best defensemen. With the Nordiques, Tremblay was very good at stopping an opponent's top scorers and even better at setting up goals. He led the WHA in assists twice.

MARC TARDIF   Left Wing

• BORN: 6/12/1949 • PLAYED FOR TEAM: 1974–75 TO 1982–83

Marc Tardif won two Stanley Cups with the Montreal Canadiens before jumping to the WHA. He scored 71 goals in his first full season with the Nordiques. He led them to the WHA title one year later.

RÉAL CLOUTIER   Right Wing

- BORN: 7/30/1956
- PLAYED FOR TEAM: 1974–75 TO 1982–83

Réal Cloutier was only 17 when he signed with the Nordiques. At the time, the NHL didn't allow teenagers to play. Cloutier showed he was ready by scoring 86 goals in the WHA before he turned 20.

MICHEL GOULET   Left Wing

- BORN: 4/21/1960
- PLAYED FOR TEAM: 1979–80 TO 1989–90

Michel Goulet was a favorite of the French-speaking fans in Quebec. He used his accurate shot to score more than 50 goals four years in a row. After his playing days, Goulet helped assemble Colorado's two Stanley Cup champions.

PETER STASTNY   Center

- BORN: 9/18/1956   • PLAYED FOR TEAM: 1980–81 TO 1989–90

Peter Stastny was one of three brothers who played for the Nordiques in the 1980s. He was a swift skater and a remarkable scorer. Stastny was the first player in NHL history to score more than 100 points (goals plus assists) as a **rookie**.

JOE SAKIC   Center

- BORN: 7/7/1969   • PLAYED FOR TEAM: 1988–89 TO 2008–09

Joe Sakic became an instant hero in Colorado by leading the team to the Stanley Cup in 1996. "Super Joe" had a hard, accurate **wrist shot**. He used it to set the Avs' record with 625 goals during his career.

ABOVE: Réal Cloutier

ADAM FOOTE   Defenseman

- BORN: 7/10/1971
- PLAYED FOR TEAM: 1991–92 TO 2003–04
  & 2007–08 TO PRESENT

Opponents who wanted to attack the Colorado net had to go through Adam Foote first. He was a clever and powerful skater who never backed down from a challenge. Foote loved to block shots and deliver hard **checks**.

PETER FORSBERG   Center

- BORN: 7/20/1973
- PLAYED FOR TEAM: 1994–95 TO 2003–04,
  2007–08 & 2010–11

Fans knew Peter Forsberg was a great scorer when he won the Calder Trophy as the league's best rookie. In the years that followed, he showed he could be a star at both ends of the ice. "Peter the Great" was a strong, smart defensive center and also an excellent passer and shooter.

PATRICK ROY   Goalie

- BORN: 10/5/1965   • PLAYED FOR TEAM: 1995–96 TO 2002–03

Patrick Roy won the Conn Smythe Trophy three times—twice with the Montreal Canadiens and once with the Avalanche. He was a cool and fearless competitor. Some believe he was the best goalie in NHL history. In 2013, he was named coach of the team.

ROB BLAKE   Defenseman

- BORN 12/10/1969   • PLAYED FOR TEAM: 2000–01 TO 2005–06

The Avs traded for Rob Blake at the end of the 2000–01 season. His brilliant defense and contributions on offense gave Colorado a puzzle piece they were missing. Blake scored 19 points in the playoffs on the way to winning the Stanley Cup in 2001.

MILAN HEJDUK   Right Wing

- BORN: 2/14/1976

- PLAYED FOR TEAM: 1998–99 TO 2012–13

MILAN HEJDUK

Milan Hejduk was a gifted goal scorer. He had a quick wrist shot and a sneaky backhand. The "Duke" led the NHL with 50 goals in 2002–03.

GABRIEL LANDESKOG   Left Wing

- BORN: 11/23/199

- FIRST SEASON WITH TEAM: 2011–12

A few months after being drafted by the Avs, Gabriel Landeskog became their best all-around player at the age of 19. He led the team with 22 goals and won the Calder Trophy.

LEFT: Adam Foote
ABOVE: Milan Hejduk

CALLING THE SHOTS

When the World Hockey Association was formed, its teams "raided" NHL rosters for much of the talent they needed. WHA clubs wanted famous names in their lineups to help sell tickets. In their early years, the Nordiques went after two of the biggest names in hockey—not to play, but to coach the team. Their first coach was Maurice "Rocket" Richard. He was a legend in Quebec, although he didn't have much experience behind the bench. Richard took the team through training camp, but he changed his mind two games into the season and quit. In 1973, the Nordiques hired Jacques Plante as coach. He stayed for a full year and led the Nords to their first winning season.

Plante was followed by Jean-Guy Gendron. He had been the team's captain as a player. "Smitty" coached the Nordiques to the **AVCO Cup** Finals in his first season. Two years later, in 1977, Marc Boileau led Quebec to the WHA championship. Quebec's most popular coach was Michel Bergeron. He built a high-scoring team during the 1980s.

Marc Crawford guided the Avs to their first Stanley Cup.

Most fans consider Marc Crawford to be the Avalanche's greatest coach. He was hired for the team's final season in Quebec. At age 34, he became the youngest winner of the Jack Adams Award as NHL coach of the year. In the team's first season in Colorado, Crawford led the Avalanche to their first Stanley Cup. He encouraged his players to keep the pressure on opposing goalies for 60 minutes a game.

In 1998, Bob Hartley took over the Avalanche. He put the brakes on Colorado's attack and encouraged a slower, more defense-minded style. Hartley believed the team could score just as many goals by being patient and waiting for opportunities. This **strategy** helped the Avs win their second Stanley Cup, in 2001.

ONE GREAT DAY

In the NHL playoffs, nothing beats having a "hot" goalie. The New Jersey Devils learned this the hard way during the 2001 Stanley Cup Finals. Their own goaltender, Martin Brodeur, had helped them move within one victory of the championship. That is when Patrick Roy heated up for the Avs. He **shut out** the Devils on their home ice in Game 6. That set up a winner-take-all Game 7 back in Colorado.

Roy was at his best from the opening **faceoff** of the dramatic seventh game. The Devils didn't come close to scoring a goal. The Avs moved ahead in the first period on a great shot by Alex Tanguay. Early in the second period, Adam Foote banged a pass off the boards to Joe Sakic, who swooped in on the New Jersey goal. Brodeur stopped his shot, but the rebound went right to Tanguay. He fired the puck into the unguarded net for a 2–0 lead.

Later in the period, Sakic gave Colorado a 3–0 lead with a goal from close range. His shot was a work of art. It went between

Ray Bourque and Patrick Roy hoist the Stanley Cup together in 2001.

a defenseman's skates and then rose over Brodeur's glove and into the upper right-hand corner of the net. The Devils finally scored in the second period, but it was too little too late. The Avalanche won, 3–1.

After the game, Sakic was handed the Stanley Cup. He immediately gave it to Ray Bourque, who had waited more than 20 years for this moment. Bourque lifted the Cup above his head before kissing it twice. "After what he has accomplished in his career," Sakic said later, "he is the one who deserved to lift it first."

With two goals and an assist, Tanguay became the youngest player ever to get three points in Game 7 of the finals. Roy, meanwhile, became a Stanley Cup winner in a third *decade*. He had already captured the trophy with the Montreal Canadiens in 1986 and 1993 (and with the Avs in 1996). "For a little boy from Quebec, I never thought that would happen," Roy said. "It is not as special, to be honest with you, as seeing Ray raising that Cup in the middle of the ice, seeing his eyes, how excited he was."

LEGEND HAS IT

WHICH COLORADO PLAYER HAD HIS NAME MISSPELLED ON THE STANLEY CUP?

LEGEND HAS IT that Adam Deadmarsh did. After helping the Avs win the Stanley Cup in 1996, Deadmarsh was amazed to see his last name etched into the trophy as "Deadmarch." It was not the first time a name had been spelled incorrectly on the Stanley Cup, but later it became the first misspelling that the NHL corrected.

ABOVE: Adam Deadmarsh's name is spelled correctly on his uniform.

WERE THE AVS HOCKEY'S MOST SUCCESSFUL NEWCOMERS?

LEGEND HAS IT that they were. When sports teams leave one city and set up shop in another, there is usually a period of adjustment. The Avalanche not only got used to Colorado quickly, they became the first team in NHL history to win a championship in the season they relocated. The only other team to do this was a football team. The Redskins won the championship after moving from Boston to Washington, D.C., in 1937.

WHO WAS THE NHL'S TOUGHEST GOALIE?

LEGEND HAS IT that Patrick Roy was. Starting in the 1990s, the Avalanche and the Detroit Red Wings had a red-hot rivalry. Many times, the two teams dropped their gloves and got into fights. Normally, goalies stay put when their teammates begin pushing and shoving—it's hard to "mix it up" wearing all that heavy equipment. But Roy liked to wander from his net. He had some legendary scuffles with Detroit goalies Chris Osgood and Mike Vernon.

Each spring, the NHL holds a player draft, during which teams take turns picking the world's best young hockey talent. To make the draft fair, the teams with the worst records get to pick before the teams with the best records. Most teenagers are happy to get paid to play the game they love; they don't care much which team selects them. This was not the case in 1991.

ERIC LINDROS

CENTER
PHILADELPHIA FLYERS

That year, when the team was still in Quebec, it had the worst record in the NHL. That meant the Nordiques owned the first pick in the draft. The best player in **junior hockey** was Eric Lindros. Some said he could have played as a professional at age 16. Naturally, the Nordiques wanted Lindros ... but he didn't want them.

Lindros told the team that he would not play in Quebec City. For a time, hockey fans wondered what would happen. Would the NHL punish Lindros? Would the Nordiques

LEFT: Eric Lindros went on to star for the Philadelphia Flyers.
RIGHT: Peter Forsberg was an immediate hit when the team moved to Colorado.

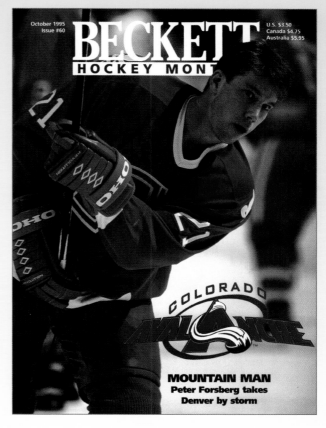

October 1995
Issue #60

U.S. $3.50
Canada $4.75
Australia $5.95

BECKETT
HOCKEY MONT

COLORADO
AVALANCHE

MOUNTAIN MAN
Peter Forsberg takes
Denver by storm

waste their pick on a player who would rather sit than skate?

The Nordiques figured out a good plan. They took Lindros in the draft and then traded him. They asked a very high price. The Philadelphia Flyers and New York Rangers both agreed to meet Quebec's demands. For a time, both teams thought they had made a deal for the young star. Much confusion and excitement followed. Finally, the Nordiques took Philadelphia's offer.

In exchange for Lindros, the Nordiques received draft picks, players, and money. When all was said and done, they ended up with Peter Forsberg, Mike Ricci, Chris Simon, Ron Hextall, Jocelyn Thibault, Steve Duchesne, and Kerry Huffman. In one unbelievable trade, Quebec went from one of the worst teams in the NHL to one of the best. Four seasons later, after the Nordiques moved to Colorado, they were crowned NHL champions.

TEAM SPIRIT

In less than 20 years, the Avalanche won two championships and built a base of fans that roots hard for the club in good seasons and bad. The Avs always have something fun happening at the arena, and the team often honors past players. In 2013, they raised Adam Foote's number to the ceiling and there was not an empty seat in the arena.

The team's mascot is Bernie the St. Bernard. A St. Bernard is a dog known for rescuing skiers and mountain climbers stranded in deep snow. Bernie wears a Colorado jersey with the number one on the back. The number is actually a dog bone. For several years, the team also had a mascot called Howler the Yeti. A Yeti is a legendary snow monster similar to Bigfoot.

LEFT: Bernie knows how to get Colorado fans fired up.
ABOVE: Fans wore this pin after the Nordiques jumped to the NHL in 1979.

TIMELINE

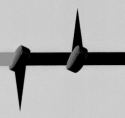he hockey season is played from October through June. That means each season takes place at the end of one year and the beginning of the next. In this timeline, the accomplishments of the Nordiques and the Avalanche are shown by season.

1976–77
Quebec wins the
WHA championship.

1994–95
Marc Crawford wins the
Jack Adams Award.

1972–73
The Nordiques play
their first season in
the WHA.

1979–80
The team joins
the NHL.

1995–96
The team moves to
Colorado and wins
the Stanley Cup.

Fans all over Colorado put this bumper sticker on
their cars after the team's first championship.

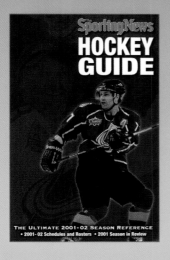

Ray Bourque got his long-waited Stanley Cup in 2001.

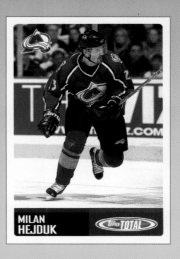

Milan Hejduk

2000–01
The Avalanche win their second Stanley Cup.

2002–03
Milan Hejduk leads the NHL with 50 goals.

2011–12
Joe Sakic is voted into the **Hall of Fame**.

1997–98
Peter Forsberg is a **First-Team All-Star**.

2006–07
Paul Stastny sets a rookie record with a point in 20 games in a row.

Rob Blake, Peter Forsberg, and Patrick Roy were all stars for the 2001 champs.

SMELLS LIKE VICTORY

When the Avalanche won their second Stanley Cup in 2001, left wing Shjon Podein didn't take off his uniform for more than 24 hours. "My dog didn't mind the smell, but my wife thought it was disgusting," he said.

SORRY, JOE

In 2011, Matt Duchene recorded his 100th point just 10 days after his 20th birthday. He became the youngest player in team history to reach 100 points, breaking the record held by Joe Sakic—Duchene's boyhood idol.

FUNNY MAN

German-born Uwe Krupp loved to drive reporters crazy. When they asked him questions, he would claim he didn't understand the language. As soon as they went to another locker, he would keep teammates laughing with hysterical jokes—in perfect English!

RIGHT: The Stastny brothers—Peter, Anton, and Marian.

OH, BROTHER!

In a 1981 game, Peter and Anton Stastny teamed up for seven goals and nine assists. The following season, their bother Marian joined the team, and the trio combined for more than 100 goals and nearly 200 assists.

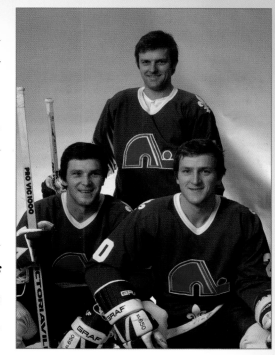

DOWN PAT

All goalies have **superstitions** and **rituals** that help them relax and focus. Before the start of games, Patrick Roy would skate to the blue line, turn, and stare at the goal until it looked smaller. He could also be spotted having "conversations" with the goal posts.

THE REAL DEAL

In Quebec's first NHL game, Réal Cloutier scored three times. Only two other players in league history had recorded a **hat trick** in their first NHL game.

SECOND LANGUAGE

Although Joe Sakic grew up in Canada, he did not speak English as a young child. Instead he spoke Croatian, the language of his parents.

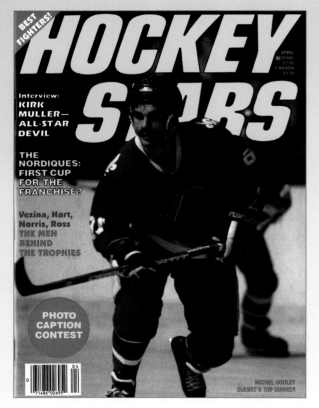

BEST FIGHTERS!

HOCKEY STARS

APRIL
$7.95
CANADA
$3.50

Interview:
KIRK
MULLER—
ALL-STAR
DEVIL

THE
NORDIQUES:
FIRST CUP
FOR THE
FRANCHISE?

Vezina, Hart,
Norris, Ross
THE MEN
BEHIND
THE TROPHIES

PHOTO
CAPTION
CONTEST

MICHEL GOULET
QUEBEC'S TOP GUNNER

"I really enjoyed the city and the fans in Quebec City. For me, to start my NHL career there … it was the best."

▶ **MICHEL GOULET,** *on his 10 seasons with the Nordiques*

"I'm not a natural goal scorer. That's probably why I pass more than I shoot it."

▶ **PETER FORSBERG,** *on why he had more assists than goals every year he played for the Avs*

"You look at both Stanley Cups, there are no bigger guys than Sakic and Roy."

▶ **BOB HARTLEY,** *on the two most important players on Colorado's championship clubs*

"No feeling is better than this!"

▶ **ALEX TANGUAY**, *on scoring the goal that won the 2001 Stanley Cup*

"We're going to have a Stanley Cup attitude."

▶ **PATRICK ROY**, *on his first priority as the coach of the Avs*

"He is a great leader in the dressing room and on the ice."

▶ **JOE SAKIC**, *on Claude Lemieux*

"On the ice, Peter was the guy that made things go."

▶ **JAMIE HISLOP**, *on high-scoring Peter Stastny*

"Enthusiasm is good. But controlled emotion is better."

▶ **MARC CRAWFORD**, *on what it takes to win in the NHL*

LEFT: Michel Goulet was truly a hockey star during his days with Quebec.
ABOVE: Alex Tanguay celebrates after his winning goal in 2001.

GREAT DEBATES

People who root for the Avalanche love to compare their favorite moments, teams, and players. Some debates have been going on for years! How would you settle these classic hockey arguments?

THE ERIC LINDROS TRADE WAS THE BEST THING THAT EVER HAPPENED TO THE TEAM ...

… because the seven players and draft picks the club received helped them win the 1996 Stanley Cup. In the years after the team moved to Colorado, several players that the team received in exchange for Lindros became stars.

THE LINDROS DEAL COULD HAVE BEEN EVEN BETTER ...

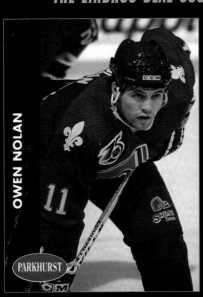

OWEN NOLAN

… because the New York Rangers were offering two future all-time greats and $12 million in cash. The Rangers thought they had a "done deal" after agreeing to trade defenseman Brian Leetch and goalie Mike Richter. Imagine these two young superstars on the ice with Joe Sakic, Mats Sundin, and Owen Nolan (LEFT). Not only would the Nords have been instant Stanley Cup contenders—they might have stayed in Quebec and built a *dynasty*.

JOE SAKIC WAS THE GREATEST TEENAGER IN TEAM HISTORY ...

... because he was already the team's best all-around player at the age of 19. Sakic joined the Nordiques in 1988–89, and by season's end he was the lone star on an aging club with a losing record. Sakic could have begun his NHL career a year sooner, but he asked the Nordiques to give him another year in junior hockey to better prepare for the pros. Sakic scored 160 points that season!

SERIOUSLY? GABRIEL LANDESKOG IS HANDS-DOWN THE BEST TEENAGER IN TEAM HISTORY ...

... because he was named captain before he turned 20. A lot of fans thought the Avs should keep Landeskog (RIGHT) in the minor leagues after they drafted him. He not only proved them wrong by winning the Calder Trophy—his leadership convinced the team to make him the youngest captain in the history of the NHL.

The great Nordiques and Avalanche teams and players have left their marks on the record books. These are the "best of the best" …

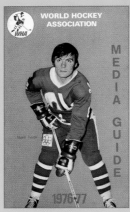

Marc Tardif

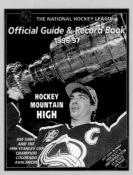

Joe Sakic

AVALANCHE AWARD WINNERS

CALDER TROPHY
TOP ROOKIE

Peter Stastny	1980–81
Peter Forsberg	1994–95
Chris Drury	1998–99
Gabriel Landeskog	2011–12

HART MEMORIAL TROPHY
MOST VALUABLE PLAYER

Joe Sakic	2000–01
Peter Forsberg	2002–03

LADY BYNG MEMORIAL TROPHY
SPORTSMANSHIP

Joe Sakic	2000–01

ART ROSS TROPHY
TOP SCORER

Peter Forsberg	2002–03

CONN SMYTHE TROPHY
MVP DURING PLAYOFFS

Joe Sakic	1995–96
Patrick Roy	2000–01

MAURICE "ROCKET" RICHARD TROPHY
LEADING GOAL SCORER

Milan Hejduk	2002–03

ALL-STAR GAME MVP

Joe Sakic	2003–04

WHA MVP*

Marc Tardif	1975–76
Marc Tardif	1977–78

WHA ALL-STAR GAME MVP

Rejean Houle	1974–75
Réal Cloutier**	1975–76
Marc Tardif**	1977–78

WHA PLAYOFF MVP

Serge Bernier	1976–77

DENNIS A. MURPHY TROPHY
WHA BEST DEFENSEMAN

J.C. Tremblay	1972–73
J.C. Tremblay	1974–75

BILL HUNTER TROPHY
WHA SCORING LEADER

Marc Tardif	1975–76
Réal Cloutier	1976–77
Marc Tardif	1977–78
Réal Cloutier	1978–79

* *Known as the Gary Davidson Award & Gordie Howe Trophy.*

** *Shared this award with another player.*

AVALANCHE ACHIEVEMENTS

ACHIEVEMENT	YEAR
WHA Finalists	1974–75
WHA Champions	1976–77
Stanley Cup Champions	1995–96
Stanley Cup Champions	2000–01

ABOVE: Valeri Kamensky scored 10 goals and added 22 assists during the team's run to the 1996 Stanley Cup.

LEFT: Shjon Podein was one of the most physical players on the 2001 champs.

PINPOINTS

The history of a hockey team is made up of many smaller stories. These stories take place all over the map—not just in the city a team calls "home." Match the pushpins on these maps to the **TEAM FACTS**, and you will begin to see the story of the Avalanche unfold!

TEAM FACTS

1 Quebec City, Quebec—*The team played here as the Nordiques for 23 years.*

2 Denver, Colorado—*The Avalanche have played here since 1995.*

3 Rochester, Minnesota—*Shjon Podein was born here.*

4 Trumbull, Connecticut—*Chris Drury was born here.*

5 Burnaby, British Columbia—*Joe Sakic was born here.*

6 Toronto, Ontario—*Adam Foote was born here.*

7 Montreal, Quebec—*Ray Bourque was born here.*

8 Simcoe, Ontario—*Rob Blake was born here.*

9 Bratislava, Slovakia—*Peter, Anton, and Marian Stastny were born here.*

10 Ústí nad Labem, Czech Republic—*Milan Hejduk was born here.*

11 Voskresensk, Russia—*Valeri Kamensky was born here.*

12 Belfast, Northern Ireland—*Owen Nolan was born here.*

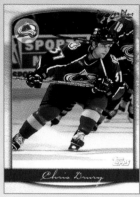

Chris Drury

GLOSSARY

ALL-STAR GAME—The annual game that features the best players from the NHL.

ASSISTS—Passes that lead to a goal.

AVCO CUP—The championship of the WHA.

CHECKS—Body blows that stop an opponent from advancing with the puck.

CONFERENCE—A large group of teams. There are two conferences in the NHL, and each season each conference sends a team to the Stanley Cup Finals.

DECADE—A period of 10 years; also specific periods, such as the 1950s.

DIVISION—A small group of teams in a conference. Each NHL conference has three divisions.

DRAFTED—Selected during the annual meeting when NHL teams pick the top high school, college, and international players.

DYNASTY—A family, group, or team that maintains power over time.

ELUDED—Stayed out of reach.

ERA—A period of time in history.

FACEOFF—A battle for the puck that occurs after play stops. Two players "face off" against each other as the referee drops the puck between them.

FIRST-TEAM ALL-STAR—The annual award that recognizes the best NHL player at each position.

HALL OF FAME—The museum in Toronto, Canada, where hockey's best players are honored. A player voted into the Hall of Fame is sometimes called a "Hall of Famer."

HAT TRICK—Three goals in a game.

JUNIOR HOCKEY—A series of leagues for players in their teens.

LOGO—A symbol or design that represents a company or team.

MINOR LEAGUES—All the professional leagues that operate below the NHL.

MOST VALUABLE PLAYER (MVP)—The award given each year to the league's best player; also given to the best player in the playoffs and All-Star Game.

MOTIVATION—Something that inspires people to achieve a goal.

NATIONAL HOCKEY LEAGUE (NHL)—The professional league that has been operating since 1917.

OVERTIME—An extra period played when a game is tied after three periods. In the NHL playoffs, teams continue to play overtime periods until a goal is scored.

PLAYOFFS—The games played after the season to determine the league champion.

PROFESSIONAL—A player or team that plays a sport for money.

RITUALS—Procedures that are done the same way again and again.

ROOKIE—A player in his first year.

ROSTER—The list of a team's active players.

SHUT OUT—Held an opponent scoreless.

STANLEY CUP—The trophy presented to the NHL champion. The first Stanley Cup was awarded in 1893.

STANLEY CUP FINALS—The final playoff series that determines the winner of the Stanley Cup.

STRATEGY—A plan or method for succeeding.

SUPERSTITIONS—Behaviors based in magic or luck.

VETERANS—Players with great experience.

WORLD HOCKEY ASSOCIATION (WHA)—The league that operated from 1972 to 1979.

WRIST SHOT—A shot taken by "flicking" the puck with a quick turn of the wrists.

LINE CHANGE

TEAM SPIRIT introduces a great way to stay up to date with your team! Visit our *LINE CHANGE* link and get connected to the latest and greatest updates. *LINE CHANGE* serves as a young reader's ticket to an exclusive web page—with more stories, fun facts, team records, and photos of the Avalanche. Content is updated during and after each season. The *LINE CHANGE* feature also enables readers to send comments and letters to the author! Log onto:

www.norwoodhousepress.com/library.aspx

and click on the tab: **TEAM SPIRIT** to access *LINE CHANGE*.

Read all the books in the series to learn more about professional sports. For a complete listing of the baseball, basketball, football, and hockey teams in the **TEAM SPIRIT** series, visit our website at:

www.norwoodhousepress.com/library.aspx

ON THE ROAD

COLORADO AVALANCHE
1000 Chopper Circle
Denver, Colorado 80204
(303) 405-1100
http://avalanche.nhl.com

HOCKEY HALL OF FAME
Brookfield Place
30 Yonge Street
Toronto, Ontario, Canada M5E 1X8
(416) 360-7765
http://www.hhof.com

ON THE BOOKSHELF

To learn more about the sport of hockey, look for these books at your library or bookstore:

- Cameron, Steve. *Hockey Hall of Fame Treasures.* Richmond Hill, Ontario, Canada: Firefly Books, 2011.

- MacDonald, James. *Hockey Skills: How to Play Like a Pro.* Berkeley Heights, New Jersey: Enslow Elementary, 2009.

- Keltie, Thomas. *Inside Hockey! The legends, facts, and feats that made the game.* Toronto, Ontario, Canada: Maple Tree Press, 2008.

INDEX

PAGE NUMBERS IN **BOLD** REFER TO ILLUSTRATIONS.

THE TEAM

MARK STEWART has written over 200 books for kids—and more than a dozen books on hockey, including a history of the Stanley Cup and an authorized biography of goalie Martin Brodeur. He grew up in New York City during the 1960s rooting for the Rangers, but has gotten to know a couple of New Jersey Devils, so he roots for a shootout when these teams play each other. Mark comes from a family of writers. His grandfather was Sunday Editor of *The New York Times*, and his mother was Articles Editor of *Ladies' Home Journal* and *McCall's*. Mark has profiled hundreds of athletes over the past 25 years. He has also written several books about his native New York and New Jersey, his home today. Mark is a graduate of Duke University, with a degree in history. He lives and works in a home overlooking Sandy Hook, New Jersey. You can contact Mark through the Norwood House Press website.

DENIS GIBBONS is a writer and editor with *The Hockey News* and a former newsletter editor of the Toronto-based Society for International Hockey Research (SIHR). He was a contributing writer to the publication *Kings of the Ice: A History of World Hockey* and has worked as chief hockey researcher at five Winter Olympics for the ABC, CBS, and NBC television networks. Denis also has worked as a researcher for the FOX Sports Network during the Stanley Cup playoffs. He resides in Burlington, Ontario, Canada with his wife Chris.